CAREERS IN
REAL ESTATE SALES

DIFFERENT PEOPLE WANT DIFFERENT THINGS from their careers. Some people value predictability, while others prefer flexibility. Some people like to be in charge, while others prefer to let somebody else make the big decisions. Everybody wants to make money, but most people are willing to settle for less income if they can get other things that they value in a career. The only person who can decide what you want to get out of your career is you.

Careers in real estate sales can be many different things. Full time, part time, self-employed or reporting to somebody else. You can make just a moderate income, or you can make millions. Work from an office or work from home. Maybe even from your car. Over 400,000 people work as real estate brokers and sales agents, and every one of them goes about it a little differently. It would be difficult to find a career that offers as much diversity.

There are two kinds of real estate sales professionals: brokers and agents. Brokers are licensed to run their own brokerages, and buy and sell real estate on behalf of clients. Agents work for brokers. Agents and brokers are often referred to as Realtors, but this title – note the capitalization – is conferred only upon brokers and agents who have earned accreditation from the National Association of Realtors, the main professional association for real estate careerists. It is incorrect to use the title "Realtor" as a generic label for all real estate professionals.

Getting into the real estate business is easy. Making serious money at it is hard. If you pursue this career, you will find that most real estate sales pros earn a solid living, but only a few have very high earnings. In a sense, you will get out of your real estate career as much as you put into the work.

Pay close attention to the information contained in this report. You will find sections on what kind of education you will need for your career in real estate, how much money you can expect to earn at various stages of your career, and even a few things you may like or dislike about the business. If you like what you read here, be sure to check out the links to associations and websites.

WHAT YOU CAN DO NOW

THERE ARE MANY THINGS YOU CAN BE DOING right now to get a leg up on your career in real estate sales. Talk to the people around you who have bought or sold real estate.

Many of the people in your life have probably bought or sold real estate, and all of them have a story to tell about the process. How about your parents? Your neighbors? Buying and selling real estate are things that most people do a few times, and nobody ever forgets the details. Just ask and you will be regaled with stories of eccentric agents, huge down payments, interest-rate negotiations, properties won and lost, inspections gone awry and a host of related issues that only come with real estate transactions. Get a conversation going. You may be surprised at how much you learn.

Few industries have benefitted from the Internet as much as the real estate business. Brokers, agents and buyers now have more information at their fingertips than ever before. Everybody knows what is for sale all the time. Geospatial mapping technologies have made it easier than ever to plot critical elements of information like crime statistics, school district boundaries, and proximity to shopping and entertainment. Calculating comparable values has never been easier, either. Log on to Zillow.com, Trulia.com, Redfin.com, or the websites associated with major brokerages like Coldwell Banker and Century 21. Take a look at properties for sale in your own neighborhood and nearby areas. Where are properties most expensive or least expensive and why?

HISTORY OF THE CAREER

REAL ESTATE SALES MAY SEEM A COMMON WAY to earn a living today but the career hardly existed until fairly recently. For most of human history, most people could not legally own land, let alone buy and sell it whenever they wanted to. The history of the real estate business is the history of property rights.

For a modern American the idea of property rights may seem pretty straightforward. You buy something, you own it. Nobody can take it away from you without some kind of due process, whether paying you for it or taking it away through legal action as in the case of eminent domain or as payment for a debt. Generally speaking, what is yours is yours.

In the grand sweep of human history this is a bold new development. For the first 250,000 or so years that modern humans have walked the earth, there was no private property. Small bands of humans wandered large areas, following herds of animals in a never-ending hunt. Nobody thought about private property because nobody stayed put for very long and everybody had to work together to survive.

The advent of agriculture changed everything. About 10,000 years ago humans figured out how to grow their own food, enabling them to stop following the herd and to stay in one place. Suddenly land became valuable, and some land was more valuable than other land. Leaders arose in the form of kings, pharaohs, and emperors who claimed authority over large swathes of land and the people who lived on it. Only the rulers and their friends and family members were allowed to own land. In Europe, these landowners were known as aristocrats. The people who worked the land but could not own it were known as peasants. Peasants often rented the same piece of land for generations but were never allowed to own it.

One of the reasons Europeans sought out opportunities in the New World was to break away from the strictures of the past. Settlers who made the voyage to America could own land by buying it from an earlier settler, or by claiming it by clearing and farming a plot that would then be recognized as their own. Cities created property markets as they grew. In 1862, the United States government passed the Homestead Act, which gave 160 acres of land in various Western territories to anybody willing to claim it and build a house on it.

Founded in Chicago in 1855, Baird Warner was the first modern real estate brokerage. The company played a critical role in building the city by helping to channel money from Eastern investors into development projects in the new and rapidly growing city. Baird Warner's employees served as agents for the investors, providing local knowledge and saving them multiple trips from the East Coast.

Responding to demand, real estate brokerages spread swiftly. One-hundred-twenty such brokerages banded together in Chicago in 1908 to form the National Association of Real Estate Exchanges. In 1916 the organization changed its name to the National Association of Real Estate Boards and coined the title "Realtor" to describe real estate sale professionals who belonged to the organization. Now known as the National Association of Realtors, the organization still uses the Realtor title, always with a capital "R."

The requirement for real estate agents and brokers to earn licenses was driven by a combination of legal and financial complexities involved in buying and selling property, and the desire of organized real estate businesses for greater professional status. The National Association of Realtors has done a great deal to standardize many business practices, requiring agents and brokers who wish to become Realtors to pass an exam.

In the 1990s, the Internet began to disrupt many of the ways in which real estate brokerages conducted their business. One of the advantages to belonging to the National Association of

Realtors was access to the national Multiple Listing Service, which was created in the 1960s. Through the MLS, Realtors knew exactly what properties were available and had easy access to details about each property, like its sales history and appraised value. This information was generally unavailable to the public, which gave Realtors great leverage over their clients. Even after the Internet came into widespread use, the National Association of Realtors tried to limit access to this valuable information. In 2005 the United States Department of Justice sued the organization for restraint of trade, forcing it to share MLS information. Today there is very little difference between the information available on MLS sites run by brokerages and on websites like Zillow and Trulia that are available to everybody.

The real estate industry has been through ups and downs in recent years. A nationwide crash in 2008 depressed markets from coast to coast, destroying billions of dollars in value in a matter of months. Although the crash was unwelcome to many sellers, it did create what is known as a buyers' market in which many people bought properties they would not have been able to afford before the crash. Times were tough for real estate sales professionals, however, as commissions shrank and many owners held onto properties waiting for the market to rebound. In most places, the market has come back. Such crashes have happened from time to time over the years. There will be more to come. Still, it takes more than a crash to stop people from staking their claim to the American dream of home ownership.

Today's real estate sales professionals are highly trained and capable. They know about finance, marketing, building codes, neighborhood schools, landscaping, and a host of other important factors.

WHERE YOU WILL WORK

EVERYWHERE THERE IS LAND YOU CAN BE SURE there is at least one real estate agent or broker ready and willing to help customers to buy and sell it. You can build a career in real estate anywhere you want. There are some important differences between markets, however.

Clearly, a real estate broker who deals in residential real estate in a small town in the Midwest is going to have a completely different experience than the broker who markets million dollar apartments in New York City. Both specialize in residential real estate. Both have to conduct their business in accordance with their states' laws. However, the Midwesterner will mostly be dealing in single-family houses with yards while the New Yorker will handle condominiums in high-rises. Their markets will be different, their customers will be different, and their incomes will be very different.

The Midwestern broker specializing in single-family houses, for example, will have to know about local building and zoning codes, school districts, crime statistics and comparable sales in the area. The New York City broker will have to know about all of those things plus be up-to-date on bylaws governing cooperative buildings – known as "co-ops" – with active boards that can screen and turn down potential buyers, and know everything there is to know about the local restaurant and theater scene, and the nearest subway stop. The Midwesterner will also likely deal mostly with straightforward mortgages and the occasional Veterans Administration loan. The New Yorker, by comparison, will have to be conversant in every kind of financing scenario, from condo conversions to cash and everything in-between.

There are also differences in commercial real estate. The Midwesterner could be dealing in everything from downtown buildings in small cities to vacant land in the middle of nowhere, whereas the New Yorker would be concerned mostly with office and retail space, with perhaps some light industrial property in the outer boroughs. In all of these cases, residential and commercial, brokers and their agents have to become specialists. Their clients will expect them to know everything there is to know about their corner of the real estate market. So go where you will feel most enthusiastic about the market. If you want to sell single-family houses in small towns, pick a small town and get to work. If million-dollar condos in high-rises are more to your taste, go to where that action is.

DESCRIPTION OF WORK DUTIES

Real Estate Agents

Real estate agents are the careerists most people think of when they think of real estate sales. Agents are often the only real estate professionals with whom buyers have any direct contact – they are the public faces of the real estate business.

All real estate agents must pass a state-mandated exam in order to work in the profession. Exams and requirements vary from one jurisdiction to the next but generally involve serious study of a wide range of topics, from finance to building codes and zoning, and many others. Many careerists fail to pass the exam on the first try and must make multiple attempts. Real estate laws and financial dealings are very complex. States have a significant interest in making sure that the people who help buyers and sellers get through the process know what they are talking about. Agents also take additional courses through the National Association of Realtors to polish up specific skills.

Real estate agents work closely with buyers to find the right properties for their needs. Most real estate agents specialize in residential real estate, and often a particular kind of residential real estate or a particular area. It is quite common for agents to become experts in, for example, single-family houses or condominiums. Most agents try to focus their activities on a specific geographical area so that they can get to know it well. Zeroing in on a few city neighborhoods or a clutch of suburban communities makes it easier for agents to keep an eye on available inventory of properties for sale, to memorize vital statistics on hot topics like schools and crime, learn the whereabouts of grocery stores and other essential service providers and, most importantly, get to know the people and institutions in the area in order to generate word-of-mouth referrals, which are critical to any agent's success. A small area is also more practical, given that agents spend many hours in their cars driving from property to property.

In a typical day, an agent may meet with several different clients to show them properties that they may want to buy. This involves meeting clients at the properties or picking them up somewhere and driving them around. Lunch or dinner may be included, and many real estate searches have been conducted almost entirely from coffee shops. Agents and clients can become quite friendly during this process, especially if it takes a long time.

Although spending your days hanging out with clients, looking at houses and stopping for lunch may sound like fun, it can also be very trying. Buying a home is a very emotional experience for most people. A home is the largest purchase most people ever make. Start with hazy ideas about years of bliss in a perfect new home, add terror at the amount of money about to be committed, and you have a very potent formula for emotional distress. If you enter this profession, you will spend many days listening to home buyers quibble over silly things like door knobs, paint colors, appliances, and landscaping, all of which are easily changed to whatever they would prefer. You will also get into the minutiae of why a home located in one place is ideal, while a similar home a block or two away is beyond consideration. You will never cease to be amazed at the number of ways in which potential home buyers can turn a simple, rational decision into the most stressful activity ever undertaken by anybody, anywhere.

Agents are required to work for brokers, who actually own listings for properties. Many careerists are happy to remain working as agents for their entire careers. On the plus side, they leave the headaches of managing a business to somebody else and have much more control over their time than brokers generally do. On the other side, they have less control over the entire process and will probably never make as much money as brokers who get a cut of the commission from every listing associated with their brokerage. Agents are undeniably the junior partners in this relationship but there is no rule saying that everybody has to want to be a boss. If being an agent provides you with the income and flexibility you need, stay an agent.

Real Estate Brokers

Many people never notice the difference between brokers and agents because they both work with clients to buy and sell properties. There are actually many differences. Brokers are entitled to employ agents to act on their behalf and to take final responsibility for all business dealings undertaken by their brokerage. Real estate brokers also own listings and get a cut of each listing, even if they have never met the buyers or sellers.

Many brokers work in the field with clients just as agents do. They make appointments, show properties, hold open houses and do whatever else is necessary to buy or sell property. The big difference can be seen at the time of a sale. Agents get only a portion of the commission paid to the brokerage they work for. They may get the larger share but they never get the whole commission, because brokers always get their cut. Brokers who handle the actual purchase or sale of a property keep the entire commission.

This is something to consider. A six-percent commission is pretty typical. A property that sells for $500,000 will generate a $30,000 commission to be split between the buyer's broker and the seller's broker. If both sides of the transaction were represented by agents each $15,000 broker's commission would then be split between the broker and the agent. These splits are open to negotiation, but for example, the seller's agent may be fairly senior and entitled to 75 percent of the commission and the more-junior buyer's agent will get 50 percent of the buyer's commission. That means the seller's agent gets $11,250 and the buyer's agent gets $7,500. It also means that the brokers they work for get $3,750 and $7,500, respectively, even though they may have done relatively little of the actual work involved in the transaction. If the brokers pound the pavement and handle the deal themselves, each gets to keep all $15,000.

Brokers have the responsibility of putting their name on every listing. Most real estate brokerages have a person's name attached to them, even if they are affiliated with a national broker chain. Names like "Bob Smith Century 21" and "Susan Jones ReMax" are very common.

Property Managers

Many real estate brokerages also run property management businesses. Most states require property managers to be licensed real estate agents or brokers. Many agents and brokers also take on some property management duties, while others devote themselves to property management full time.

Property management companies typically take over the day-to-day management of properties from their owners. Homeowners who need to move away for a few years due to a career relocation but intend to return to their home in the future often contract with a property management company to rent their property while they are away. This is also a common procedure for real estate investors who buy properties in order to rent them at a profit. The owners sign a contract with the property management company that gives it the right to advertise the home for rent, vet potential tenants and attend to routine maintenance. Most property management contracts contain an option that awards the company a commission if a tenant buys a home while renting it. Property management companies also manage multi-unit properties like apartment buildings and condominiums.

Property managers handle all of the duties typical of a real estate agent, from showing properties to potential tenants to handling the paperwork that closes the deal. Property managers usually work on a commission basis and get a cut of the rent for each property for which they find tenants. If you pursue a career in real estate sales, you may have the opportunity to do some property management.

Appraisers and Assessors

If you are interested in real estate, it may be worth your while to look into careers in real estate appraisal or assessment. In simplest terms, appraisers value real estate for property owners and real estate brokerages, while assessors value real estate for local governments in order to assess property taxes.

Requirements to become an appraiser or assessor vary by state but most states require appraisers and assessors to possess a bachelor's degree and earn a certification or license. To become a certified general real property appraiser, for example, requires 300 hours of classroom training and 2,500 hours of work experience.

STORIES OF REAL ESTATE SALES PROFESSIONALS

I Am a Residential Real Estate Sales Agent

"You have no idea how many miles I put on my car in a typical year. I can do 30,000 miles a year without trying, and I rarely leave my home turf of a handful of suburban communities on the edge of a major city. With a car, a laptop computer and a cell phone I am good to go. Oh, and a coffee shop. I close more deals in coffee shops than anywhere else. Absolutely necessary for the real estate agent on the go.

I love my job. First and foremost, I am happy to be out in my community and doing my best to promote the virtues of living here. I like the flexibility that allows me to do important things like drive my kids to soccer practice and run errands during the day. I really like the fact that I can make good money on a flexible schedule. I've never had a better job.

I majored in English in college. Not because I wanted to sell real estate but because I liked it and didn't know what I wanted to do. I started my career in public relations but drifted away from it in my 20s after having children. When my kids got a little older, I started looking for a job that would allow me to control my schedule and make money. Real estate was the obvious choice.

In a typical day I will meet three or four different clients and show them properties that might meet their needs. This requires doing hours of homework. Clients can go online and get all sorts of information about available properties, and they often ask me to show them particular properties. They also expect me to come to them with suggestions. I usually know the area better than they do, and that's what they pay me for.

Most clients go into the home-buying process with a smile. Still, it can get very emotional. Many people expect to walk into their dream home right away. It rarely works like that. Most people just don't know how easy it is to change things like colors and appliances, and even to move walls. I always encourage my clients to look not just at what the home is now, but what it could be.

To show a vacant home I only have to show up and let the clients in. Properties for sale have lock boxes on their doors with combination locks available only to real estate agents and brokers. Homes that are occupied are a little trickier, as I usually have to call ahead to make sure the current owners have time to clear out for half an hour or so while I show their home. It can be a logistical headache, but mostly it's fun. There are certainly worse ways to spend my days."

I Am a Commercial Real Estate Broker

"I started out in residential real estate but burned out very quickly. For many people buying a home is simply not a rational process. I worked with some clients for months, showing them hundreds of possibilities and putting in innumerable hours for nothing. It didn't happen often, by any means, but just often enough to rub me the wrong way. I'm just not wired for that process.

That's why I got into commercial real estate. My clients are all working professionals who know exactly what they need and why. Some of my clients are real estate professionals in their own right who are responsible for acquiring real estate for their employers. Large companies often employ real estate professionals, especially when their business requires regular real estate transactions. Fast-food companies, for example, buy thousands of properties for their restaurants and employ their own staffs to do it. When I work with small companies, I often deal directly with an owner or other senior executive. They may or may not know very much about real estate but they know exactly what they need to make their company go.

This business is very nine-to-five. Nobody is running errands on company time. Everybody wears a suit. On the other hand, we don't work evenings or weekends, either. Residential agents and brokers work whenever their clients need them and that often means nights and weekends. My commercial clients work during regular business hours. Yes, it's more formal but it's also more predictable. I am paid a salary plus commissions, which is different from residential real estate.

Commercial clients are interested in things like square feet, proximity to highways and airports, up-to-date infrastructure for office networks, ample parking for employees and customers, and proper zoning to do whatever it is they do. They also have individual needs that can vary greatly. A law firm may want offices in a prestigious office building, while a manufacturer will need a huge space with loading docks and room for heavy machinery.

I don't just show properties. I help clients to find everything they need. For commercial real estate that can mean looking into research reports to determine if a particular property will provide the kind of foot traffic required or has the proper visibility for customers. Legal issues can get pretty complex for commercial property, too. You just can't open a factory in a downtown business district. By the time they come to me, most clients have done a bit of homework and know what they need, more-or-less. They count on me to give them the details."

I Own a Full-Service Real Estate Brokerage

"I work for myself. I wouldn't have it any other way. I have held pretty much every position in the real estate business and always knew that I wanted to end up as the owner of my own brokerage.

I started in real estate while I was still in college. I majored in business administration and had always found real estate to be interesting. I took a couple of classes in real estate finance and entrepreneurship while I was in school and signed up to take my state's real estate agent exam as soon as I could. I passed on the first attempt and by my early 20s I was working as an agent for a local brokerage. Keep in mind that my schedule was part time in those days. I was juggling my career with going to college, which wasn't easy. Still, the flexibility offered by a career in real estate made it possible.

I passed the broker's exam a few years later. Owning the listings was a huge leap for me. I made more money but I also took on greater responsibility. As a junior broker, I worked for a brokerage just like an agent. My commissions were bigger than an agent's, and as a broker I got a cut of all of my listings, but I was still an employee and had to fork over a cut of my commissions to the brokerage.

It took about a decade for me to gain the experience and confidence I needed to start my own brokerage. It's not enough to have some capital and sign a contract with a national brokerage. Establishing your own brokerage requires deep, deep knowledge of the area you want to serve. You need to have contacts everywhere, from the chamber of commerce to the local school districts to the police department and every civic organization out there. Real estate is the most local business there is. My brokerage is affiliated with a major national brokerage, as most brokerages are. The national brand gives me a familiar name and logo and access to their databases of listings and leads. It's much harder to go it alone. I hire agents and junior brokers on a commission-only basis. That means they only get paid when they sell properties and I only keep them on my team if they sell regularly. They carry my name on their business cards.

I enjoy what I do. I won't kid you, though. Being the boss isn't all power and glory. I have to look after accounting, marketing, human resources, paying the utility bills, and every other aspect of owning and managing a small business. I also spend a lot of time showing the flag. That means I go to innumerable civic association meetings and spread my name around. I shake hands, pass out business cards, sponsor a Little League team and do a lot of other things that are absolutely necessary to keep the brokerage's name in the public eye. I want to be the first name that comes to mind when people in my area want to buy or sell a home. Mostly I like it, but there are days when I wonder why I ever stopped just being an agent. Some days I never get to sit still."

I Am a Residential Property Manager for a Real Estate Brokerage

"My brokerage does everything. We have divisions devoted to residential real estate, commercial real estate, and even foreign real estate. We also have a division devoted to managing properties. It's a logical extension of our core business of helping clients to buy and sell properties.

I was a real estate agent and broker for many years before I started in property management. Most states require property managers to be licensed real estate professionals before they can go into property management. Most brokerages also require property managers to take courses from an association like the Institute of Real Estate Management or the National Association of Residential Property Managers. Managing a property has much in common with real estate sales, but it's not the same thing.

My company signs contracts with property owners to take over their properties and manage them in return for a cut of the rent. Most management companies take a 10 percent commission on every rental, some of which goes to the agent who signed the lease. We have a wide variety of clients, from single-family homeowners who need to keep a house rented for a few years until they are able to move back to it, to investors who just want to hold onto properties and make a profit on the rentals. We manage everything from single-family homes to large apartment complexes.

Just like a real estate sales agent, I spend a lot of time showing properties to potential renters. I also meet with property owners to sign contracts. Unlike a real estate sales agent, however, I maintain a relationship with the property owner and renters after the deal has been made. My company collects the rent and takes care of routine maintenance. As far as the tenants are concerned, we are their landlords. They never meet the property owners. We manage everything.

This is a fun job. I still do some real estate sales but most of my time is spent managing properties. For me, the real estate business is the real estate business – owning, managing, buying, and selling. It's all part of the same fascinating business and I'm glad to be able to learn as much as I can about it."

PERSONAL QUALIFICATIONS

MANY PEOPLE THINK THEY WANT TO GET into real estate, but most of them would not be very good at it. To be successful in real estate sales you should have outstanding customer service skills, be patient and flexible, and have a good head for business.

For most people, a home is the biggest purchase they will ever make. People save money for many years in order to come up with the down payment for a home. Then they have to make sure they can afford to live in it. This requires making a monthly mortgage payment, paying utility bills and seeing to maintenance, lawn care, and a never-ending list of other responsibilities that come with owning a home. It should come as no surprise that people are emotionally invested in the purchase of a home, and can be fussy to the point of irrational. They will decide to buy or not to buy a home based on irrelevant things like cabinet knobs or the color in the living room, both of which are easy to change. They will get excited about things you could never predict, like a shady spot in the yard just right for a hammock, or a sunny spot just right for an herb garden. Your customer service skills have to be the best to handle these responses.

The process requires patience and flexibility. Many of your clients may not make sense to you, at least not until you have spent some time with them and know them. Patience is definitely a virtue for real estate sales professionals. Flexibility is closely related to patience. Most real estate sale professionals work odd hours in order to meet the needs of their clients. Most people work during the day, meaning they are free to look at properties only on weekends and in the evening. That is when real estate agents and brokers have to work. They also need to be flexible when it comes to meeting the needs of clients. It is not uncommon for residential real estate buyers to change their minds many times during a house hunt. A couple who starts out looking at homes in the city may drift into the suburbs, or vice-versa. That fourth bedroom that was so critical early in the search may not seem so important if it can be swapped for a bigger garage. Clients learn about themselves and their desires as they progress. Agents and brokers need to be able to learn along with them.

Real estate sales may be an emotional roller coaster but it is also a business. More than half of real estate brokers are self-employed, and most agents are independent contractors who also make their own decisions. If you want to leave the chores of business administration to somebody else, real estate is not the career for you. You will be doing your own accounting, advertising, marketing, sales, taxes, and even rudimentary legal work. It is not as hard as it sounds but some people do not look forward to running a business.

ATTRACTIVE FEATURES

REAL ESTATE IS SUCH A POPULAR CAREER CHOICE for many reasons. Most real estate jobs are very flexible, which makes them especially attractive to people who have other responsibilities, like families. Real estate careers can also be very lucrative, even given the flexible hours. Most real estate agents are independent contractors who manage their own time. They may be affiliated with a brokerage, but most brokers let agents run their own shows as long as they produce and do not do anything to harm the company's reputation. This means that agents can take care of important duties like getting the kids off to school in the morning, and then spend the day attending to real estate business.

Most agents spend their days showing properties to clients, prepping homes for open houses, going to the brokerage office to pick up promotional materials, and many other tasks related to selling real estate. Along the way, they find time to go to the grocery store, pick up dry cleaning, and maybe have lunch with a friend (who might be a prospective future client). Then they can be home when the kids get home from school, have dinner with family, and pop out again in the evening for an hour or two to do a showing for clients who are not available during the day. It is a busy routine, but for many people, it beats sitting in the same office cubicle all day.

More than 90 percent of all American millionaires made their money in real estate. Like most people, you have probably been conditioned to believe that millionaires are movie stars, professional athletes, and captains of industry. Many are, but they represent only a tiny fraction of people with more than a million dollars to their name. Plenty of regular people have amassed significant wealth through real estate. Real estate is the most reliable investment around, even with the occasional market downturn. There are also several ways to make money with real estate. You can buy an apartment building, for example, and rent the apartments for more than it costs you to maintain the building. Along the way, your property may increase in value, which gives you additional profit when you sell it. Just owning a property gives you equity, which you can use to make more money. Most real estate agents and brokers also buy and sell real estate for themselves. That can produce income in addition to their earnings from commissions.

Commission rates vary depending upon factors like seniority and type of property, but agents generally earn between three and six percent on each sale. Sell a property for $500,000 and your commission will be anywhere from $15,000 to $30,000. Close on a sale several times a year, and you will reap a good income.

Real estate careers can be enjoyable. The best agents make themselves pillars of their communities. They join the chamber of commerce. They go to civic meetings. They sponsor floats in Independence Day parades. These efforts are all about marketing, but they are also a rewarding way to spend your time. You will be out and about, making friends and making deals. You will find something to look forward to every day.

UNATTRACTIVE ASPECTS

THE TRUTH IS THAT MOST REAL ESTATE CAREERISTS never break into the big time. Dedication is a must if you want to make it big. Being a one-person show and being able to make your own schedule is a real perk, except sometimes it is not. Squeezing personal errands into your work day is definitely an advantage, as is the ability to take the occasional three-day weekend without asking anybody's permission - but flexibility is also a necessity. Clients are not usually available to look at properties when it is most convenient for you. You work for them, not the other way around. This means that you need to be available when they need you. For residential real estate agents this usually means working evenings and weekends. People with regular jobs just are not going to be able to meet you at two o'clock in the afternoon on a weekday. If you want to make a sale you will have to meet them when they are available, which means after work and on weekends. This may not sound like a problem now, but when you have a family it can become a real headache.

Real estate brokers and agents specializing in commercial properties do not have to worry about working evenings and weekends so much because their clients are mostly professionals who will look at properties during the workday. Commercial real estate careerists work normal daytime hours like most other people.

Although many people are lured into real estate by the promise of making money in a relatively low-pressure, casual working environment, most of them never make much more than an ordinary living. Making big money requires consistent application of effort. Many real estate careerists take too much advantage of the informal aspect of the career. They get started late, take long lunches, avoid civic functions and do their best not to work on weekends. There is not anything wrong with this scenario, but it is not a recipe to make big money. If this is what you want, that is fine. Maybe you have kids or other commitments that are more important than high income, but if you want to make millions you will have to work hard for it.

The most successful real estate agents and brokers treat their career like a full-time job. They set regular hours and stick to them. If their clients need them in the evenings and on weekends, they aim to please. They may extend their flexibility to necessities like picking up kids from school or going to medical appointments, but they do not take two-hour lunches or wile away their afternoons at the mall. They circulate, they hand out business cards and they make follow-up phone calls. They usually do it without supervision. For many people this may be the hardest part. Success will be up to you. You will have to be a self-starter. Nobody will make you do anything.

EDUCATION AND TRAINING

GETTING INTO THE REAL ESTATE SALES BUSINESS requires training and education. Specific requirements vary from one state to the next, but at a minimum aspiring real estate agents and brokers need to be at least 18 years old, have a high-school diploma and pass a state-mandated exam. Requirements may also vary from one employer to the next, with some brokerages happy to hear from anybody who passed the test, and others looking for candidates with bachelor's degrees or some other credential. How far you want to go with your education and training is largely up to you.

Most states require aspiring real estate brokers to spend a few years working as real estate agents before they are eligible to take the test for a broker's license. Some may waive this requirement for careerists with certain academic credentials or relevant professional experience. It makes sense, however, to work as a real estate agent for a while before making the decision to become a broker.

Passing the required exam is critically important. You cannot pursue this career without passing your state's mandated exam. Some careerists take the exam several times before passing it, while others study hard and breeze through the first time. Buy a good study guide, take an exam prep class, and hang out with real estate agents. Do whatever you have to do to pass the exam.

A bachelor's degree is recommended. Even though a degree is not usually required, there is no denying that earning one will give you a leg up in your career. Some brokerages only hire agents with degrees. They want agents who are smart, knowledgeable and who have proven that they can learn. They may also want agents with degrees because they believe that such agents will do a better job of relating to their customers. This is especially true of brokerages that do business in upscale neighborhoods and in commercial real estate sales.

More importantly, earning a bachelor's degree is an excellent opportunity to learn things that will help you in your career. Many colleges and universities offer business administration degrees with concentrations in real estate. From a business perspective, real estate is closely related to finance. Real estate curricula also include courses in basic marketing, management and accounting, all of which will be useful as your career progresses and becomes more complex. A bachelor's degree in business administration is highly recommended, even without a concentration in real estate.

While in college you should not pass up the opportunity to complete an internship. An internship is a job related to your major that takes the place of classes for a summer or semester. Most internships are paid and they all come with innumerable opportunities to learn about the field you think you want to enter. Interns work alongside working professionals. They make coffee but they usually do some real work, too. Either way, they get to spend quality time learning how their dream career really works. Many recent graduates get their first real jobs from the companies where they completed an internship. On the other hand, a few interns return from the experience and change their major because their internship showed them that their dream career was not so dreamy after all.

Some real estate careerists go on to earn Master of Business Administration (MBA) degrees in finance or real estate. This is a decision you can put off until after you have been in the business for a while.

Will you want to become a broker? You will have to pass another exam. Becoming a broker means you can set up your own business and hire agents. It also means that you get a cut of every listing that comes through your brokerage. Not all brokers set up their own businesses. Many join existing brokerages and become partners. Either way, they take on responsibility for the full range of business functions, from hiring and training new agents to devising marketing campaigns and keeping an eye on the books and bank accounts. This is another decision you can make a few years down the road.

EARNINGS

YOU CAN MAKE VERY BIG MONEY IN REAL ESTATE. You can also earn a perfectly respectable, middle-class living and enjoy the perks of working as much or as little as you wish. You can make a career in real estate sales pretty much anything you want it to be.

Most real estate agents earn about $50,000 per year. Brokers earn slightly more, on average. This may not sound like much, but it behooves you to keep in mind the fact that many real estate sales professionals are part-timers, happy to make some money in a profession that allows them to devote more time to other things. Real estate has the potential to enable careerists to make more dollars per hour than they can in almost any other part-time job.

Real estate agents and brokers are paid on commission. That is, they get a cut of the price of the property being sold. Commissions vary widely, as do the arrangements made between agents and brokers to share them. In simplest terms, listing brokers start the process by listing a property for sale on a multiple listing service, or MLS. Six percent is a fairly common commission, paid by the owner who is selling the property. If the listing broker sells the property, he/she gets the entire six percent of the sales price. If the property is sold by a buyer's broker, the commission is split between them. This is the most common arrangement.

Keep in mind, however, that real estate agents work for brokers. If two brokers split a commission but the buyer's broker was represented by an agent, the buyer's broker and agent must split their half of the commission. Let's say that a property sells for $500,000. The six-percent commission of $30,000 is split between the listing broker and the buyer's broker, with each receiving $15,000. The sale was actually made by an agent working for the buyer's broker, so the buyer's broker and agent must split the $15,000. This arrangement is open to negotiation. Some agents start out earning about half of the broker's commission. This figure rises over time as agents gain seniority and make more sales. Senior agents generally get to keep about 75 percent of the commission, but this arrangement varies from brokerage to brokerage. In this hypothetical scenario, the agent would be paid $7,500 with a 50-percent commission and $11,250 with a 75-percent commission.

OPPORTUNITIES

REAL ESTATE SALES CAREERS ARE PERFECT for self-starters who are willing to innovate and broaden their horizons. If you want to get ahead, you can earn additional certifications. Certifications vary by jurisdiction but, generally speaking, there is always room for growth. If you are an agent, become a broker. You will be able to hire agents, get listings and keep a piece of the commissions earned by the agents who work for you. Just the opportunity to set up a full-fledged business could be enough of an attraction to move up to broker status. Most agents work from their homes and cars and do not employ anybody. If you want to join the top ranks of the profession you will have to become a broker sooner or later. Most jurisdictions also require agents and brokers to earn different licenses to buy and sell commercial real estate. This is also an excellent way to make your career more interesting and, potentially, more lucrative.

Whether you need an additional license or not, you should always be willing to get outside your comfort zone and look into new types of real estate and different markets from the types of real estate you already work with. Residential agents, for example, may find it refreshing to dabble in commercial real estate from time to time. Commercial real estate transactions are generally completed within the context of a larger business. The people doing the buying and selling do so during regular working hours, which can be a nice change of pace after sacrificing your weekends to holding open houses. Commercial real estate transactions also tend to be very straightforward affairs quite unlike the emotional hand-wringing that often comes with the residential side of the business. Savvy businesspeople are interested only in location, zoning, square footage, and price. They know they can paint the walls any color they want.

You can also consider entering new markets. This can mean a lot of things. Many residential real estate agents specialize in relatively small geographic areas or even specific cities or neighborhoods. This is a good way to get to know the market and become familiar with the issues most buyers will ask about, like schools and crime. It can become routine. Why not check out a different area? Look for listings in areas with which you are not very familiar, or even for listings in your area that are in different price categories than those you usually deal with. If you sell middle-class houses to middle-class people, you can always try your hand at affordable housing, or go the other direction and try to list and sell a mansion. Each market offers its own challenges and opportunities.

GETTING STARTED

GETTING STARTED AS A LICENSED REAL ESTATE AGENT is relatively easy – gaining momentum is the hard part. Study for the exam. Once you pass the exam, make sure you have a well-written résumé to make your case to potential brokerages.

Nobody can get into real estate sales without a license. Requirements vary from one jurisdiction to the next but every state in the country requires real estate agents and brokers to be licensed. In most states, anybody who is at least 18 years of age can take the real estate agent's exam. That does not mean passing it is easy. Each state's requirements are a little different, so it behooves you to get a good study guide for your state's exam. Such guides are readily available, and many are now online. A study guide may cost a few dollars but do not hesitate to spend the money. The alternative is failing the exam. Without the certification you have no future in the real estate business.

Once you have your license you can begin sending résumés to brokers in your area. Most major metropolitan areas are home to hundreds of real estate brokerages, all of which employ multiple agents. Some employ small armies of agents. This is because it costs a brokerage nothing to hire an agent. In fact, agents often have to pay fees to sign on with a brokerage. The fees cover things like business cards, promotional materials and any in-house training required of new agents. Very few agents are full-time employees of the brokerages they work for. Brokerages allow agents to use their brand and get listings through the multiple listing service. In return, agents sell the brokerage's listings and share the commission. It is a symbiotic relationship that benefits everybody.

When crafting your résumé be sure to list all the jobs you have ever had and emphasize any duties that involved sales and customer service – retails sales, fast-food sales, for example. If you have never sold real estate before you cannot pretend to have any experience. You will have to convince a potential employer using your related skills.

Once you have a contract with a brokerage it is time to get to work. Do not wait for the opportunities to come to you. Seek them out. The more you circulate in your community, the more word-of-mouth referrals you will get and the more money you will make. Most real estate markets are clogged with casual part-timers who are happy to stay that way. There are always a handful of superstars. With some effort you can become one of them. Good luck!

ASSOCIATIONS, PERIODICALS, WEBSITES

■ **Apartments.com**
www.apartments.com

■ **Bomi International**
www.bomi.com

■ **Century 21**
www.century21.com

■ **Coldwell Banker**
www.coldwellbanker.com

■ **Georgetown University School of Continuing Studies**
www.scsonline.georgetown.edu

■ **Home Ad Net**
www.homeadnet.com

■ **Homes.com**
www.homes.com

■ **Hubzu**
www.hubzu.com

■ **Institute of Real Estate Management**
www.irem.org

■ **International Living**
www.internationalliving.com

■ **National Association of Realtors**
www.realtor.org

■ **National Association of Residential Property Managers**
www.narpm.org

■ **Neighborhood Scout**
www.neighborhoodscout.com

■ **Prudential**
www.prudential.com

■ **Real Estate Institute**
www.realestateinstitute.net

■ **Realtor.com**
www.realtor.com

■ **Realty Tech**
www.realtytech.com

■ **Redfin**
www.redfin.com

■ **Remax**
www.remax.com

■ **School Digger**
www.schooldigger.com

■ **Sotheby's**
www.sothebysrealty.com

■ **Trulia**
www.trulia.com

■ **United States Census Bureau**
www.census.gov

■ **University of Florida**
www.ufl.edu

■ **University of Illinois**
www.illinois.edu

■ **University of Phoenix**
www.phoenix.edu

■ **University of Southern California**
www.usc.edu

■ **University of Wisconsin-Madison**
www.wisc.edu

■ **Yahoo! Homes**
www.homes.yahoo.com

■ **Zillow**
www.zillow.com

www.ingramcontent.com/pod-product-compliance
Lightning Source LLC
Chambersburg PA
CBHW061237180526
45170CB00003B/1338